or, on being the other woman

or, on being the other woman

SIMONE WHITE

DUKE UNIVERSITY PRESS / DURHAM AND LONDON / 2022

© 2022 DUKE UNIVERSITY PRESS
All rights reserved
Printed in the United States of America on
acid-free paper ∞
Designed by Matthew Tauch
Typeset in Alegreya and Alegreya Sans
by Westchester Publishing Services

Library of Congress Cataloging-in-Publication Data
Names: White, Simone, [date] author.
Title: Or, on being the other woman / Simone White.
Description: Durham : Duke University Press, 2022.
Identifiers: LCCN 2021048042 (print)
LCCN 2021048043 (ebook)
ISBN 9781478015826 (hardcover)
ISBN 9781478018469 (paperback)
ISBN 9781478023067 (ebook)
Subjects: BISAC: POETRY / American / African
American & Black | POETRY / Women Authors |
LCGFT: Poetry. | Prose poems.
Classification: LCC PS3623.H578874 O766 2022 (print) |
LCC PS3623.H578874 (ebook) | DDC 811/.6—dc23/
eng/20220204
LC record available at https://lccn.loc.gov/2021048042
LC ebook record available at https://lccn.loc
.gov/2021048043

Cover art: Photo by Dana Scruggs. Courtesy of
Dana Scruggs Studio.

Love is contraband in hell.

—SAIDIYA HARTMAN < ASSATA SHAKUR

or, on being the other woman

heaped therefore residually heaped

beside myself on the bed next

i fetch my son's pretzels, but prerogative

lingers upended could poweR's lengths

also belittle me between your visits am i

belittled am i less   pure

semiologists pressed me toward

an apparent residue cRowning evident or

    almost?

we go to the room for stories, nestled

lumped or thrown together we and things

for very little children Camden worrying a razed benefit engineered a loop a figure

    eight an on-ramp a mother hacking for UbeR pink and pink and the tiny pitchfoRk

    he and i discover in the side of some plastic grass an instrument's use bears a direct

    relation to our activity in observing

its constructed unpile

monitoring a stink Bug's progress, or, beautiful random application of remorseless violence: there. my boy has begun to apprehend such concepts as affection, better identified as interested longing, does this one like me? maybe he doesn't like me? lOok the Buug-h. windy undifferentiated consonants unsorted words please me so. one day i will tell how much time was there before he could evoke in me anything like interest. his thought interests me, i date from discussion of the need to use a pot or toilet for shit. in a few days i would fall into a rage on the street arguing with my mother on the telephone.

what makes me if her desire vibrates as pleading packed in insult

in my guise as woman work and insomnia
rumble through they are girders money
worries girding my whole body such job
interviews
sayjng intoleraB
le
kinds of nothing about how all of it came
to pass
is this about money? my inability to pass into the moneyed upper-middle class to which i had been "raised" / projected? one thinks one has refused, i really hate liberals, i do not like to hear the troubles of middle-class persons fussing about their children's use of cell phones.

what if i misdirect or misuse what i now know about the feminine crucible? my boy inquires about my anger, somehow knows it is for / against something not him at all, just wants to know what. you don't like Eli? no, no, i like him, i'm sorry i . . . mostly i have
Been

able to decide what aspects of my own potency my child will witness

when i break ties with men or refuse to keep with the tradition of fungibility

iNsofar as my action is a lump of mass action or it is insanity, such as to choose to act
    precisely in emotional ways

the emotions are the cortex of reason

then my heart tells me the way

as there is no way

my boy and i rely on media to keep me strong enough to love

i like science fiction because

Something terrible is going to happen

suppose it is "the ocean" under this Boeing belching white whatever you say, mommy, ok
  okay

Oceanic will come over all these very rich their big boats, "houses," and so on will come
  over all this mess

see, "reality" instead turn over tones of words ending in *-ull* that lose their significance
  and exactitude within seconds

a casualty of brain injury and exhaustion, both, is memory loss

you split open part of your head and for six months repeated words you had already said
  but i didn't say

anything out of delicacy or tenderness or timidity

i didn't say why the fuck are you still working

what possible conditions could exist that require you to work without shelter while your
  brain swells

who iS your wife

come home the terrible thing

//

Du BOis teaches radicalization is possible.

adolescent boys living temporarily in my home, one like my own child, my brother's
son, these words might have meaning for someone reading, like my own child, regard
it as an undifferentiated space in which to pile expensive junk reeking of petrochemical
deodorizers,

losing track of devices they need all these power sources and stations to connect

my need for certain kinds of privacy, tidiness, results in occasional inability to share per-
sonal space, surely related to believing that i am pursued or overrun by half-eaten food
empty water glasses bits of poop lining the rim of the toilet seat (at some point, cleaning
a toilet seat, i'm like, is pee corrosive?) unmatched socks of others i must compulsorily
clean up

in early life among loud, not-gentle, numerous family of origin, later, the men with
    whom i shared my homes,

each deeply silent, somewhat still.

i'm not revolted by evidence of the lived lives of other people.

effective means of housekeeping categorically interest me.

the pleasures of a clean/orderly house . . . there are few absolute pleasures.

as my life gradually became too busy to properly clean my own home, i paid another
woman to clean. Patricia cleans my house now, even while I am away, working in an-
other town. she watches so the boys don't harm anything they have not been warned not
to harm.

the fight with my mother about the boys' occupation.

i negotiated a decent rate of pay in a tenure-track job at the University of Pennsylvania.
more than one person in my family accused me of being "angry and frustrated" in the
space of one week, but i feel saner and more fulfilled than ever. "height of my [emotional]
power." for a week, i shared my bed with my son. we arranged for five days together in
two cities, not New York, after many months. my ex-husband made taunting sounds at

me in my house in front of my child while i kept eating a piece of pizza and waited for him to leave. i received the first copies of my new book.

don't try to explain that i have changed. i don't feel much when people call me names or the functional equivalent. miserable, delusional, immoral.

i have things a sense of things that belong to me that i have clung to such as an apartment. possessions, while they are not a mathematical index, can focus the instincts and point toward

what must be sacrificed.

these five tones Rae Sremmurd emit a melodic noise
i've never heard anywhere Swae Lee is composer prince of melancholy being related to
 sex and money which way it slants
overtop each outcry, could you repeat once more the urgently communicable passions
of us. the only thing i can think of like it is the emoji that shows the silly face leaned to
the left, laughing and crying, belief in the single or primary nature of space-time falls
therefore out of its place, drops off comically in a drool. comedy is thus cruel regarding
the dual opportunities presented by catastrophe such as stroke.
every time Juicy J shows up on a track now there is some comedy in it,
viz, "you say no to ratchet pussy Juicy J caint."
i ran for forty-five minutes, concurrently i worked out a pretty nuanced system for
talking about powerGlide. trap has developed as a means figuratively to represent in
and beyond words (oo, oo, oo) an emotional notation system for desire in our lifetime,
one specifically attuned to the horror whiteness performs in the presence of black men,
the absolute goal of US sociality is to securitize interior persons and monies against the
threat of the aliveness of them, which is not lost on anybody
let them speak for themselves
what means therefore to recall very precisely how pussy pops or why it would pop for you
 why is this funny
trying to think of a poetic instance outside lesbian feminism
 i always put my pussy
 in the middle of trees
 like a waterfall
 like a doorway to god
outside the figure also, also outside a system of diamonds or gold teeth or strippers or
rapturous marriage
i cannot think of a single poem, someone else will know and write to me in disgust
using language to say

when at last i am with you again and you begin to press yourself inside me

an inch or two at a time

i am so relieved not to be myself and never want to be myself again and have felt grateful

for all the ways i have aged, my vagina has aged, all of me seems to have lived up to now

as pathway

for what passes through us

i have used this music, its metaphorical aliveness, as a proxy for the unbearable ways my

body declares itself irrepressible or central to anything that is. i think

about the ways this might be wrong, or how, Dag asks, to think an ethical way of being in

relation to the black men i know and do not.

i continue to fail to propose to the *New York Times* an essay on the role Meek Mill has

played in this, if this could be a way of activating others to refuse the possibility of incar-

ceration for living.

//

What is the relation between pleading and womanhood?
is how the problem came to me in the night.
caution has set in regarding language proposals, compositional possibilities
attunement to deep activities of the mind is still hot
i should not speak wantonly even freely of my theory of externalization
nor forget i am the subject of opinions and whispers; that i have given up total privacy
in writing about the real conditions of my life. it is some kind of shock to be of the order
and also talking about oneself.
relays, circuits leak in physical and metaphysical terms
others would burn us at the touch-point if there were empathy
it is so much worse than that it is ever ah ever missing an orbital alignment being a
        woman slices me out the dimension of men as if i might write to him always ah
        something devastating the chime of "the erotic vibrations of the speaking body"
forces are not requests
such requests as between what i conduct physically i see myself attempting with my
palm to rotate the fields between us so as to open his understanding
is it to me or to what i fill up that is not death? this i attribute to all the ways i have
        become a woman
as way
orientation with respect to any outer worlds that might be
also time's hatred of the possibility of responsiveness the action of time as ritual against
        as such plea or exposure
to wall a person in
block

//

got me a real mistress and she independent

—GUNNA

i have bexome misaligned or crooked with respect to the field

of dependency basic

Ally a free radical

if i keep looking at the word *independent* i can see it surrounded by practices of sex work

it is always pussy that gives me value and this, fact of undeniable facticity,

must also enter my estimation of the state of my own excess. the forms my life takes

have berserk intensity.

dissolute facticity

whatever means i use to accomplish liberation will lead inevitably to the destruction of

someone's marriage

that's true

"you rail against men"

my lover writes to me we use an encrypted form of digital messaging as if anyone cares

    what we say to one another certainly i do not believe that anyone does but these are

    his wishes

men as they exist in their bodies are not the subject of my interest so i do not "rail

    against" them

that is a misrepresentation of the whole of my aesthetic and phenomenological project

which involves taking up the vision i have been given of my own freedom

i have been given a vision of it, life beyond use

the white women who own the fancy nail salon i go to fired the manager i loved, a black

    woman photographer who treated me with professional respect, respect for my

    time, my lack of it, she knew my work and the work of my sister, she let me use my

paid-for seat as a place to weep behind the screen of her conversation, using herself
    as a blessed covering for me; i realized,
those bitches don't want me in here
i understood i had witnessed an act of aggression against our presence, our desire to be
    adorned, to have comforts, to cultivate the rot of this corruptible
all its death-y glory
the nigger woman is the mistress of the world
optimal dependency being a flowering of sexual and other forms of competition

indeed the field articulated as has been is a mode of transit to and fro in a determinate
    plane a machine

parallelism

slide, even, a thought that allows for the permanent possibility of trajectory

when what arrests, contracts, seizes time in time

swallows, causes the secure ego to become anxious

the round back of pouncing animalia

my swooping compatriots

& all prey

movement unsafe and disorganized in this beautiful quantum wilderness

these are the materials

note the absence of wind from where i am

hunched in the kitchen

awaiting the return of my child, i blow smoke through rigged-up exhaust and wonder, is

this further evidence of having lost control of the present?

that winds do not blow back my smoke upon me?

am i so

off-course to the natural world?

my boy's prepositional weirdness tells the substance of his growth which i approve

i, too, obsess on basic shit

more so wishing to be overtaken by heavenly voices

dark and deep talking to me anyway

none other than the god of say, Precious Lord, i did not know that aperture god though i

know the blank intimately this day, this filament god come through on very small air

//

woke up coughing
feeling exposed feeling something must be in my throat
coughing
feeling unsure about the nature of observation
i had already been warned
i would affect the aggregation if i refused

i had always been afraid of what would happen to me if i could not learn to control my
strangeness
i thought of the ways i had been helped by the women
the women who had helped me
had i poisoned (what was the agreement i
had made? had i agreed?
is that what had happened?

i would not call it despair

this feeling i have stumbled upon a nameless register of social life riven by the human
power to withdraw care

the pulses are of love, awareness of one another being passed on and through
we speak of sound as a place where this aspect of the known world becomes intelligible
and worship it there the great woman poets (Notley especially) provide nothing though
i look to them also in love when i suspect i am in the wake of a collective jolt; that is
moving away from the consequence of my little war to be absolute or blind in the way i
protect my sense of where there can be life

the women who had helped me who refused help

for my own good or refused to speak with me because i don't exactly know why
contamination because it is already too hard and they had already decided about the
little war not to be in its violence which i was bringing to us? to them?
the cost of being strange has something to do with the energies of these women their
power to cut me off

the declarative sentence of the last generation of woman poets

now nearly overtaken by doubt about the singularity of the action female

very young women i teach struggle with the genre of words that constitute the feminine

    penumbra's

thought afterlife

Do this Do that

we do not recognize ourselves in an attitude of defiance that proffers patriarchal regard

sometimes i feel sorry for anyone who has not reached the conclusion that solitude is too

    pregnant a state to be rightly associated with desire

"This is the beginning of a new / spiritual and ethical position. For a woman. Based on

the supposition of harmful intent— / that another, male or female, even without realiz-

ing it / might very well want to hurt me, cause my subjugation."

that these lines exist is meaningful, Notley says words i see as effecting a response in me

that is *assent to belief*, conduction of the response *yes*, all my flesh

knows she is working one-on-one level with the words to put them down as the force she

feels in tension with the release of her gifts

"meditate in separate closets" these small rooms into which we carry defensively the

hope not to be subjugated

not to be harmed

feel sorry / yes they mean to harm you, Alice

in my reading this week Linda Brent appeared and another Linda

the second giving advice about child support Do This

Do that but i cannot bear to be told what to do. i sustain a lifelong peace with my best

    friend who says, you do not have to be in so much pain what other choices can you

    make;

peace depends upon minute or incremental degrees of detachment from what must be a
momentary thrill to subjugate the one in need
of advice. a subtle ethical difference.
i feel sorry for anyone who does not think of the garret, little boxes, places to think as
tiny dungeons where synapses learn later to remember your being enfolded in a tight
place
hidden and hiding
Did Linda Brent suffer from chronic pain because her body began to attack its memory
of meditating in a separate closet? An autoimmune disease?

when at first it became necessary to work away from my boy, necessary to spend days
        away from my child because i was working to make money for us, he was very small
        and not the kind of child to be carried about
in some ways an unmanageable baby, inflexible
the weight of our attachment would lift as i moved away from him in space
emotionally it was neutral as i had not the resources to have any joy away from him only
        anxious detachment
enough to make possible our going on together as we are, i, being his mother
now he is a little kid and i have taught him what words to say if he must call me to him.
he abuses this privilege calling out "mommy, i need you" whenever i am out of his sight
Because he is experiencing new fears inside our apartment, I come slowly when he calls,
but I answer immediately. He never need wait to hear my voice.
to be without my boy will never again be a matter of being in solitude. too much has al-
ready happened. i meditate, then, on the ways in which my solitude is being hidden and
hiding or being held away. is, in other words, involuntary.

i could no more abandon my love to instructions

feminism that instructs

i have to break off as i write of the sensation of being without my child

it makes so little sense to speak of it

i suppose i can arrest temporarily or for a long time my waiting

to be reunited with him

to choose never to return, to have him taken away

we are then in a realm of absolute violence

not self-care

bald survivalism

i have been nearer to the gestures of mere survival than i would like and would not
    import them to my dreams

softening toward defiance as the tax on its maintenance is so extreme

At Your Best You Are Love

I must next texture the generative energy of this poem by writing what I know about our love. To loop in genre identification and emotion can dictate what is next, what causes what.

I call myself ethically to account for "dependency." I brought this term to describe a quality of femininity from which I have broken, not by choice, yet broken absolutely, anyway.

To account for opacity I sense in the poem that is not from "art" or "privacy."

"*I want to be empathetic.* █████████████████████████████████████ ██████████████████████████████████ *the only rule I've had* ████████████ I *will not hide or lie.*"

I closet myself in order to protect you.

Is this true and in this, have I done right?

I do not know whether knowledge about sexually inflected dependency (the economic emotional and racial matrix that forms black women as persons who carry, fuck, never tire, and remain impoverished) is related to knowledge about who this writing is for and what i am in offering the writing what is the kind i imagine for myself, in bidding as i do where monetary uncertainty is the same as begging.

If I am writing a script, it is a script for performance of the intellectual status of the art professional

If it is an epistle, it travels no distance

because of the way you are with me and yet are not of this world

We cannot now lop the letter off from the Messiah

As texture, writing is as we are

Investigation in a compositional attitude characterized by supplication or doubt
selecting can be the only verb with adequate power
technological operations are infused with each creature's adequacy to the vibrations
I love to think of riding and being ridden
by constitutive quanta
I have experienced this with you bodily and also being admired on the street
as black love is metaphorical, therefore shocking
with you, i have been
inventing a manner of experiencing the end of my life under this dispensation
I have not meant any of the meanings of every word they say
it is not clear you have not meant them or understand
how i hold off the figure of my sex in my mind to get between the figure and love

in my graduate seminar on the materiality of black womanhood, we were in the room
cowering at words we know for describing things. i think i felt fear in the room; but
maybe i am odd and make others feel odd when they must yield the floor, because i am
the teacher, to the hesitant language i drop into. i think the unfitness of words is the
base from which we might understand such concepts as barbarity, the crudeness of
words, their impingements
such rough modifications as we make
sweep violently through empty space
can we see acts of caring for one's sane self, the skinless remainder that i must be in inti-
macy with my loves or attuned to the needs of my child or truly to discern
what is called thinking

as helplessness
where writing is as we are
my time is not the same as your time already
that time was not on me symbolically or otherwise, it is only like clothes to me, it brushes
on me more or less and can keep the elements off my body if that is what i need in order
to survive an interval

Figure 1: that other time as an ugly garment made of what would decompose but for innovation in methods of slaughter and preservation
on the workhouses
I am, you, we are dependent
each word a slaughterhouse
we go to be enclosed

I struggle with the idea of outside daily, my faith in the possibilities for existence outside my own formation little more than a trickle most days, even on occasions when i consent to being, for you, what I appear to be.
I understand this as giving but you do not understand it to be giving, perhaps because it is not possible "to give," more likely because what I am supposed to be cannot give choose decide

in our love a variety of embattlement that approximates my fundamental struggle to live and thus to change / is an embodiment of the life-struggle within or inside—with you i see my life-struggle eroticized—outside (Figure 2: a darkness of true interminability until the end, until a thing comes into existence out of it)—this struggle being math-ematically impossible with respect to dailiness—while mothering is a compound of dailiness and striving with the physical material with which i have to work—our love, as pain, appears as a high form of aridity that presumes nothing

i think about gayl jones. once in a while i read all the stories i can find about gayl jones her early books her *corregidora* her husband who cut his own throat with a knife in their house in Kentucky. why was gayl jones living in Kentucky, wait . . . i always ask myself the same question and i don't look it up and i'm not going to find out now either. In the night, while i am lying awake for two or three hours, panicked about money or the loss of my lover or worrying about congenital alcoholism, i see before me a grieving and blood-splattered gayl jones led away by police, in handcuffs, to a psychiatric hospital.

i want to talk about abandonment.

i don't believe poetry or writing or love want death from me. rather—my son began using this word *rather* in the last two weeks, so i am sensitized to beauty in iterations of being *in stead*—rather, i am cheered by the absolute indifference of the universe to my desire. A long time ago i gave over to godlessness; that is, there is no god but there is something like division or departure or rapture that neither begins nor ends each time i am abandoned to an irruption of understanding.

months spent agonized and dumb end suddenly in a text message that includes the phrase "this weird distance between us" wherein i learn of the distance as such or have suddenly language for
the helical structure of my own madness
which has danced comically in my body as passionate enjoyment of a form of intimacy i
    had not been taught to hope for
Our love which is for the genius of one another the mysterious arrangement of your power of sight and of listening (your blindness to the most basic rules, too, of matrimony and divorce, i love and laugh about, in my own being subject to those rules and knowing them by rote because i was trained in the law by the ruling class and because i

have felt the power of the state come down on me, if only as infant/incident to my father, the criminal,

a man maximally disinterested in fairness)

passion twinned with disdain for the not-knowing of men, not-how or nohow patriar-chal ignorance

Of how my child's clothes are bought,

When i say your white woman lives on my back and this becomes true again and again

Again the distance which routes your belonging in the public world as a man

is the end of me

So that i Cannot be at all

Within its embrace / in your arms

my love, for all these reasons, i did not want to be a poet

If i have anything like a materiality, see, i experience it in the discovery of how "distance" means between us, and disturbs the thing i am, with all things. my "spirit," which i have abandoned to you, cannot writhe at the door of that other world. I am outside that world, i have tried to tell you in this poem. I have been put out of it and put myself out of it in love for you and with you.

. . . the beautiful woman who is also the monstrous laboring beast . . .

—JENNIFER MORGAN

Instead of persons
swirling about me
machine sounds
since i began to know myself as a person thus to attempt to craft a surface that could be
"like" inside

the vision i have of myself as a woman coming by way of this poem, inside which seeing changes; the poem's time, both long and never, the poem surrounds or bends or encircles the characteristic of being one, penetrates and moves through dense singularity to contest its interpretive and material primacy. The poem is separate from and is constituted by the interpenetrative, not metaphorical possibilities of the works that surround it, not metaphorically.

The poem is and i am surrounded by this thing;
That it is a matrix of gorgeously humane vulnerability to nonlinguistic materials such as sine waves, how we catch and are simultaneously damaged by the groundwork of aliveness;
not me and not the poem though It may be formally and discursively impossible to demonstrate their difference.
(what have i said about the figure to distinguish it from the symbolic?)
The music does not "make me feel";
the poem is an account of how I am the songs and they are me, although I do not make them and cannot and the songs say they hate me, anyway, although I must and do love them, and are even so the truth of the surround.

or, an exploration of a certain aversive possibility in or foreignness to one's own crea-turely survival, which is where I am locating or living in blackness and in my life as woman.

What can be and is done to me—then by me—because of what Future means. It's beside the point what I "think" about trap music. Trap music calls out to bodies within its range at a level of materiality that is on the register of horror insofar as it combines what black people call soul with the history of being worked to death. It is not my problem that it doesn't call out to you; where are you, then, in the places of the human with which it is in contact, which it touches and creates, where does feeling originate? Another name for the black present, which is the present, or *timespace*, or the dimensions; it is for me to breathe or not breathe, continuously, air.

//

When I say "the grind of my work," such a grammar injects the possessory with work

or loads the possessory with its laboring double, troubles the foregone conclusion of

the alienation of work, a signal change which has been predicted and pointed to as the

shape of our time, yet I am unable to speak or write of it

Only to feel as evidence of this time's being

Against contact permitting only

Making money and wounding

An Excursive feature of my own being in speech

Of the nature of the poem

Is to admit the manner in which the Trap has required me to pretend to believe in sexual

difference in order to become intelligible but the machines

ever obliterate a sui generis feminine they corrupt sounds so as to produce

As sexual becoming

masculinity that flourishes, is shined or brought piecemeal into fullness

By absolute prostration to patriarchal ambition

Thirty-five years ago i was a girl

And I have survived maturity as

the beautiful woman who is also the monstrous laboring beast

Or, After many false starts the cheapness of the way you had been making love to me

Was greater than impressionistic

//

Sh!t

This is an empty track whose bass 808/kick drops more than thirty-five seconds in
Mike WiLL's 808s are characteristically "low" and melodic
But this is one of the lowest i've heard and the most . . . evacuated. The bass line doesn't
play through on a continuous loop. Bass establishes a rhythmic shape around which
Future initially calculates his momentum, so we hear alternating presence of "musical"
bounce and what Future conveys or suggests as physical/linguistic presence (saying/
meaning) to us by moving and inviting movement in tandem with the bass's structure

When MWMI sucks that 808 out of the beat (sometimes quickly killing it in the mix,
sometimes slow decay, also, reinitiating with drag)

it becomes a model or idea that proposes the total cessation of sound beside which
Future is agitated to vocalization/celebration

[*Woooooooouh*]

As a problem of art/expression i look at that holler as falling out of the embrace of the
sounds that are holding/carrying his embodiment of speaking, riding a roller coaster on
the way down, emotional space that's opened up for him by way of the stillness that is
represented when MW stills that wave.

A while ago, I started watching beat deconstruction videos on YouTube. I don't like
the kind that aren't made by the producer/artist but someone mimicking the machine
actions they believe the producer has taken—by way of reference, the latter type is the
equivalent of transcribing an improvised solo on a traditional instrument: these are the

notes. In a "Black Beatles" video produced by Genius, the lyrics site, Mike WiLL talks about producing a rideable wave of bounce. He's talking about understanding the song in terms of its physical properties—*bounce* is a word for bass, Mike WiLL's trap bass, whose low-frequency sound waves are very big sine waves (i think of an engulfing curve that is nondirectional and therefore multidimensional, large enough to disturb conceptions of forward motion)—the entirety of a beat propelled by bass sounds is therefore spatially indifferent to forward movement at the level of experience with its edges determined by the particularities/borders of the other frequencies the producer includes.

We inhabit its total shape as momentous.

What Mike WiLL achieves with the snaky synth he wraps around that 808
When Future keeps saying *Nigga you ain't [ ] shit*
That is what Du Bois knew about Washington
Trap bass as architectonic unit
marks responsiveness to indirect-ion and passivity in the activity of building myself
"singleness of vision and thorough oneness with his age is the mark of the successful man" says Du Bois
the snakiness of the synth, it grows
Or builds out the foundational response of the nerves' impact with the initial boom
Adds complexity that invokes the possibility of separating who ain't shit from who is the successful man
those tiny tones race up out the wave as genre/kind   identity
Mike Will can shatter the bind between the 808 and the high hat; it's part of his genius so that we tingle with difference in matter-ing
this is not "musical"
The report of the wave form affects too the sexual division I have never actually experienced, I have never known myself marked as otherwise than
a man of the time, I could never but be open to
Let us call it a melodic activity in misogyny

Where the activity of the voice and all my openness to the way the voices of Trouble and Future enact
In their huffing and distortion the possibilities inherent in human presence in sounds/ that middle range of intelligibility where we walk the earth

//

Aye

a great deal of puzzling forgetting loomed or was a pall of disorientation occasionally
pierced by incompletely appreciating mental acuity   it having been possible to remem-
ber facts and feelings   in a previous period   previously   without

hesitating so gravely   not being able to speak

I inhabited time densely and so was not dead or deadened
more an aliveness or supposed anxiety that did not turn attention away
neither trembling nor luminous   it was dense or had mineral qualities
nothing of ethereal or heavens except its mean dust

several combinations of not being able to articulate the names of objects first
panicking   or shock   being puzzled coming later in relation to initial awareness of
heretoforeuncontemplated blank spots both biological, that is, neurological
not knowing the names of people or places or things in front of my students when criti-
cally sleep-deprived in the first instance

and poetic   objecting to the ordinary or orthodox way   access to words had been
described as a matter of grammar Steinian as a matter of disability stuttering   having
many words and unable to find them   also performance of ease with respect to writ-
ing metaphorically invention or creativity organized in terms of access to this kind of
speech

morbid fear of flying occasionally flares up   attributable to early incomplete under-
standing of the phenomenon of wind shear as a child gathering a plane could be hurled

to the ground by the air deducing   air travel cannot be completely safe a plane or engineers not being able to respond mechanically to the force that carries the plane   the principal absurdity of being unable to overcome physics in this basic way   how fucked we are

thus i imagine air disaster mass death and my own death to be related to a kind of unresourcefulness or lack of creativity with respect to language   or language's pathetic nature in the face of dimensions   what to call

flayed vestibularity which sounds very dramatic   Chief Keef's "Save Me," for example if Chief Keef has Asperger's i'll be a monkey's uncle
two kinds of multidimensional imagining have been troubling during the time of this work

I misunderstand *grinning* for *granny*, *warring* for *want wreck*   it doesn't matter after all if looking at a painting or listening to music that doesn't have words I misunderstand it's considered a function of excess of interpretability works having vectors operational vibrations outside their physical presentation   in common understanding   not only black people's theoretical proposals

by virtue of being in proximity to my peculiarity the speech of another   what comes out of the body of another now   more likely a long time ago then almost dying there until it is activated when I come to it   that is the things that actually die that we make perhaps going wrong

not understanding War   including the sound of a person's spasmodic coughing as a vestibular element   once the fundamentals of the so-called beat are established and the other effects some horns some amplified weed pulling all of which can be heard on any device i think it's interesting that the auditory register of the coughing is lumped into a bar with the 808 drop impossible to hear seconds later the sound signaling pulmonary illness or distress   ancillary to vocal strain

no one arrives with the intention to suffocate   *pee look darker* I hear as *pen[uh] darker* the gathering or clearing in which verbalization will begin to take place is already jammed up warring being on the mind of this man whose lungs can't fill up with either smoke or air   he says nothing grunts or counts

saying nothing technically   imagining a gnarled or entwined figure in which all the intentions of love are activated all its disappointment hovering as a fundamental magnetism in the gaps where two bodies do not touch where perhaps the hips of two persons attached the genitals form the angle at which two human bodies move away from one another this is also a space of containment   so a formation in the physical world of particulate refusal   its essence isn't contamination having a problem associated with its physical properties toward destroying the connection its hold is touching too much rather than too little   little language being necessary any first-person declaration involving *will not*   the sculptural gap between the bodies in terms of the recurrence of the figure a total imaginary   sometimes filled with nothing but disdain for the other will i guess it is domination   the point's ultimate nonlinguistic origin or location in the explosion inside empty space of the wills that takes place at an ante-material level before any kind of sex between the figures could be considered sex really being a consequence of the wild inexplicable space   the gap having an aesthetic quality that is my own understanding to make of living in the future or in other nightmares unrelated to any kind of writing

anyone living in disproportionate awareness of the chaos that is the gathering of intentional speech within the possibly violent dance of being gathered as minimally two   they spitting and accusing one another in the gap that both holds them and defines an impossible difference it's unclear how this could be heard as nothing what the man is saying is a declaration of total war and so exactly :)   the man being an innovator and also a threat and aggressively misunderstood as a matter of general agreement to be not saying anything whether or not the man believes himself to be writing and is consumed as a messenger

imagining i get into trouble personally sometimes it is possible to avoid the viciousness of white people often because of money only in the middle of my life apprehending myself my gender as a different kind of target   when T says *a nigga can survive* he isn't talking about me

taking getting into trouble as an idiom i would be into a posture of warring at this time that can be ignited by disrespect   the twitchy readiness into which i have grown standing in the kitchen listening to War i want to affirm I hear this man saying words   his life is so strong and reaching me   let me survive without stealing

When he dies he cannot be buried beside white corpses.
His neighbors have barricaded their porches against his view.
—W. E. B. DU BOIS

Go to Jail

months later   only able later   for many months holding the image of myself in the
kitchen   an image of raising up out of the nothing feeling which isn't not feeling at
all   i don't feel nothing   i feel
like i want to strangle somebody most of the time
Seeing seeing, the image, as an energetic problem of not being raised up, too
junky and at the ready i'm saying
up and above the vagueness of knowing togetherness   there we were together learning
the spiritual and the literary should never be confused
I am not in my body

acts of holding   not exactly trying to resolve how it is i am involved in Chicago's war
though I'm interested in anticipating a certain kind of moral demand

"pussy how you warring" is meaningful to me in its digital strike or pluck that covers
the time within which it becomes instantly possible to gather
as the high frequency is withheld the passion is in the stinginess of the strike   the tease
There are two definitional proposals with respect to the high hat in that song, I'd say
one allowing it to become "drill" this is "refrain" or pattern
the other proposing singularity or arrest
something incredibly stupid or bad in that plinky anti-loop

it curls up around the spasmodic coughing from which it is technically and sonically apart

and the completely undanceable horror of *this Aiki pack*

no one stops dancing

I am holding close to me Mei-mei's voice with me at all times when i am thinking
different problems with working or beginning with the nonrelation between me and them
always making an excuse for feeling close scuttling away

dancing is not an endorsement of violence but of course it is

when dancing, holding also the problematics of uplift i do feel spread out
i feel helpless and resent the sense that separating myself from feelings of love and
        enjoyment for the sake of so-called liberation is fucking us all up

Do i know myself to be a person who is stalked? AM I a killer

I can barely stand the convergence between Mei-mei's *Stars* book and what I am trying to
say about feeling empathy

you try to hold onto the visibility of this object and its location

just as unbearable
when the object is a form of personal power

Now I'm close.

You're laughing at my orgasm joke but it's not a joke. I ain't joking. From which I have
learned. To be irresolute.

//

no man has ever not tried to steal from me
that's wrong
the man who never tried to steal from me never wanted to be with me like that
while the man i was with who explicitly stole from me was so crazy at the time i didn't
think much of it,
structurally, or, i could not think structurally at the time

in california prairie light and scenes from midwinter day were coming to me in a confus-
ing way via social media

i wrote to laura, "i had a dream in which i was overcome or beset by a kind of erotic
storm, encircled by lovers; that is, men of whom i would say fucking is eternally in the
nature of our bond, the transmutational properties of masculinity . . . the three . . .
forcefully whipping around me having become a cosmos of presence to myself
mimesis with no share of the bearing down
inside their fucking gyre I transmitted
A signal for help but it could not escape because the force of the dimensions which they
were or were creating
Was a black hole
The real blackness of the hole was true I woke up knowing what words to say
Say the dream < laura

within two or three days

I had been trying to identify the name of the pressures. No i cannot remember what any
of them had done to me I try to remember forming an intention;
now I am going to act as crazy as possible and threaten to go to his job and tell his mama
    and his best friend what kind of person he is and how he has been stealing from me

all these years and telling people i am a spoiled bitch because i have all these degrees
and won't take my baby out of private preschool
So I was acting crazy and smoking out the window of my house screaming into the gar-
den at the mourning doves looking at me like i was crazy

I stopped when he said a number I guess I can't remember much about it because i got
pretty drunk afterward and woke up in the night thinking lord i am not able to do this
much longer please let this man see
My humanity

In two or three days also i had learned there was no name for the pressures it was the
most ordinary black womanhood which is not nameless has all the names of us and is
nameless and has no intention and is strategic

One of the days a young dancer came up to me and said i don't know how to embody the
musical problems and i said, well how does it make you feel
I began to be able to speak of it myself when i felt myself growing more graphically male
Through its practice
I listen at deafening loudness in my car, clearly i am trying to hurt myself
the words they say; they have a newness. I promise never to speak the words in my
poems not in defiance of interpretation but because they are so creepily hostile and un-
funny the interior they assume in address so murderous i don't see the point \ of repeat-
ing them

this is what words do

How does it make you feel? You are not allowed to have feelings you are not allowed to
have anything, and when you have something, somebody will try to take it from you,
don't doubt it for a second,

there is no honor in patriarchy it is a drug sometimes i allow my eyes to roll back in its
vicious pleasure
I can feel joy if I remember
I am feeling the power of myself as a vacuous thing
An unknown thing

Out of which words come under pressure begin to make new

So that the structure of the poem was falling down around me as were the constitutive
energies of what i was, such as they were visible or detectable to me
I sensed them breaking they were already broken; this was the condition of which the
poem must consist
The radiant materiality of circuitous attacks some such as might be deflected others
helplessly slip inside what is"

I am an ignorant fucker. difficult to be close to in that i am unsentimental and intimate with everyone. This is connected to the problems I am working through regarding meta-phor. As a form of patriarchal control over language and a currency of poetic power.

My ex-husband calls me an "ignorant fucker" when I complain that his hugely pregnant white girlfriend, who I do not know who I tolerate since for the last month and indef-inite future my son must live in her house two days in a week, cannot show up unan-nounced in my child's classroom where I pay all the bills and I watch and half do nothing and half help in the acquisition of literacy and reason. I say this is no place for this white woman; she is a free rider on my labor and love for my son. I will not support any white people with my work. I tell him all of this pretty loudly. He calls me an ignorant fucker. Now you are street? What, are you going to punch her in her face? I have fought exactly three people with physical violence in my forty-six years of life. Two men. And my sister.

"Pain—expands the Time— / Ages coil within / The minute Circumference / Of a single Brain—" "Pain—has an Element of Blank—"

I
Am
An ignorant
Fucker—
I've learned a lot from Eileen. Lay claim to the processes of your mind, deal in the mania-cal properties of the oscillating sign that is the mark on you like black is on you but don't let them force you to sing. All BUrning prerogative.

"Since a Rack couldn't coax a syllable—now"

EMily talking shit. Vs. me "being" " ignorant" "fucker"

What "is" is is   determining the terms of exaltation, praise, and defilement, the turning off and on of the pleasure and pain centers. Subjectivation.

Profanity's nonce forms engage linguistically in what sound people call muddiness, profanity's imbrication with epithet is a richer form of meaning making that taps into sign at a zero level, incredibly powerful, elementally so.

"fuck that mumbling shit" : "you are an ignorant fucker"

what has to be said beyond off/on : good/bad; what happens when a linguistic field is generated by high energy signs across a flat plane of signification—there's no need for logical progression or . . . "narrative." Each word or phrase can function as foregone, forethought, already known; that's a black ontological truism that trap music knows deeply. That's its language game.

On the one hand we experience a unidirectional surge (Playboi Carti, "R.I.P.") and on the other intense confusion via harmonic scrambling (Future, "F&N," or the new music like Lil Baby, "Word on the Street").

I am an ignorant fucker wherein the comedic shock of the thing resides in the manner in which I do not resemble and yet am the thing, impossibly misperceived

This is like this. I regard this as baby work. Ultraconservative pandering. I seek to dwell outside the figure in a zone of "Pain"

This is my country. What is the difference between the figure that destroys and the figure that breaks away i think in units of $1k

Each thousand allocated in a disorganized manner to the rubbish heap of my debts and obligations.

This is a maintenance unit distinguishable from a unit of basic economic safety

however, i reject the notion that it is unrelated to survival

Derived from the extremity of my educational status, though not a direct result

       mechanisms through which debt is incurred include education but can also

    be related to depressed wages   wage differentials wages in bureaucratic delay (90

    days is an eternity to wait for a thousand dollars)

    a bad child support regime   a regime   the entire lack of a system of affordable

    childcare or safe and effective public schooling

for black children

bourgeois expectations regarding generational wealth is a secret killer; that, and the fact

the class war rages for decades

beyond the first money

norms of gendered responsibility and financial dependency through marriage are

plainly dangerous

i wish grown people of all genders would stop talking to me about their fucking spouses

ima start asking

HOW MUCH MONEY DO THEY MAKE

don't this nigga see me working?

I think ($1k)

i would not trade my law degree for anything tho

Harvard Law School taught me to look at the ruling class look at my marginality to it

i dealt myself into an art world where there was no bohemia

Excepting its "secret" ruling class remnant

economic violence is a term from which i feel dissociated I dissociate my self from its use
being so far from poor, only desperate, i cannot see how violence
encompasses my calculations
or the irregularity of 1000 dollar transactions
2x 1000 is debt service of two distinct types
one-third my take-home pay
each time i make a thousand dollars
it's time to pay back-tuition
if i gig hard enough i'll catch up this year

Income appears to me in fast-moving sheets of $1k
Given my deficit and the way I bust ass, I can spend eleven thousand dollars in a month
on the ledger
my mind is never blank it is on
the next check

don't these niggas see me working
lol the irregularity of my thought   my vulgar 1000 dollar functions

Pope.L walks into a room. Hair looks good. Everybody knows Pope.L's hair be looking dry and wild but maybe Pope.L's supposed to be unkempt. Pope.L walks right up to me, has something to say important, not conversational, not in a conversational tone he starts talking in an urgent manner. I do take note of people's appearances, most every-body's in the way when they come up to me to say something, I don't pretend not to look. Pope.L starts talking to me like we're familiar so I figured I forgot and knew Pope.L from before but I never forget a face even though since I gave birth I can't remember shit I can't recall words like I used to. I like to characterize my thinking as orderly if baroque recklessly minute in its particularity so being unable to recall words feels like psychosis but is just aging. I asked my mother about it and she said you should get some sleep. Pope.L starts talking about how the room isn't right. And I'm thinking, what do you want me to do about it? But then I realize he's tryna be conceptually helpful like artists are helpful and nice to you sometimes when you have a good idea but it's   poor poorly conceived in terms of materials and they start building you a new setup verbally or as if conversationally they could make your concept more adequate. It is like watching some-one reach into your organs. (I don't know what this would look like but I have some imaginary stock from a C-section and my dad eviscerated in an ER; the dark hilarity of those traumas in residue.) One time Jace with the Nosferatu fingers of one hand casually manipulated a track I had cued up on my laptop, exposing or imposing his information on the things, the track and the software, too dumb for him, he appeared to crush the machine as he barely contacted, barely saw or only saw with his fingers, its interface; he revealed the sense in which my blundering was beneath him. I have always found the revelation of my ignorance to be a tremendous relief, coming into maturity or full womanhood and to terms with my lack of ego with respect to my slowness or neurological difference and somatic delight in the genius of others. But I'm what you call noncompetitive. Jerry used to say, "you are a profoundly dialectical negro," but he was mistaken. I think I have actions of contemplation that oscillate about that which is unspeakable. My mind is prostrate with respect to discursive positions. Pope.L's bemused stage-whispering. Pope.L's dirty water given to running, given in general to who would drink dirty water. Pope.L's hair was laid / I couldn't stop wondering wtf happened to him. He was talking about the "layered amphitheater of performance" or that is my language but it was coming out of Pope.L so I accepted it as that which is or was delivered of study

Pope.L was close up and in my face
Kind of berating me over a balcony rail
in an amphitheater
Lol
Ghostlike, Pope.L comes toward folks on this tier of the balcony; it is inexplicable but nobody except me is freaked out everybody else is "audience" which you wouldn't think meant dead to the world but apparently it does because this motherfucker has hereby floated and people are in no way upset. Maybe I'm upset by his tone or the pretense of exchange/dialogue without taking into account any of my prerogatives. I'm like, damn, I AM AN ARTIST.
Lol. Pope.L is certainly a better artist than me, just saying.

Often, actually, exchanging an article such as of clothing. My stinky denim shirt. My scuffed boots for yours, brother. Your potted daisy makes me howl with inappropriate laughter. I love flowers so much, yet I'm a terrifically bad gardener. Kofi texts from Mississippi about the cotton gin and I resist saying anything to him about the Beasley because he seems too bothered by seeing the machine out in the field to entertain that kind of thing. Pope.L's choir fucked me up, though. Pope.L kills frequently.

The question of can I or can't I take part in the performance really involve myself in it as the space of the amphitheater has tripled, emphasizing the way Pope.L exercises control over the problem of perspective by staying up in my face. We are off to the side of the actual stage where people are looking but I'm beginning to suspect um

"You need to commit more dramatically to the source of the conflict." I feel I'm being patronized.

WHICH FUCKING CONFLICT

"I have to pick up Isaac. What I have to say right now is that I love being a woman. I have loved coming to be her although it is not at all glamorous."

I don't like techno at all, I keep saying I don't like house music people ask what about Detroit what about Baltimore. I don't care about techno I truly do not. Increasingly I don't like jazz, the major public practitioners freak me out. I like Anthony Braxton; that's not a musical thing. I am very interested in electronic music and what DJs make when they stop "playing clubs"—I am interested in black people and electronic music. I am interested in Jeff Mills.

//

Two particles that make a continuum or ideal, in how the space between
them relates to a third event, / as how clouds against a windowpane
admit space that continues to a cloud on the mountain, / a sheath of a
space of feeling in the material sheaths of her body for perceived order,
depend / on your having felt the relation.

——MEI-MEI BERSSENBRUGGE

poetry, that which had never failed
failed
all i invented were new ways to arrange things as time On my nerves
every word they say another source of fucking chagrin
in poetry as life, forms appear meaningless before my anger. i cannot find "a logic" aside
from straight dope capable to pierce the exactitude of pure rage. losing the original
thread or intention of the poem emotionally or its having spent itself in encounter with
its Master emotion

Who are you? WHy are you in my life? What have you to do with me and the child?

a study of Berssenbrugge
A study of Chief Keef
such that for several days i worked toward blending various techno-discursive aspects of
the noun *gorilla*, the noun *time*, I recognized a multidimensional order of the ape and set
about organizing how i wanted others to experience that point
It made a lot of sense
My lover in his life and work suggested to me the possibility of promulgating this kind of
information through machines but I had not the skills; i told him so. insofar as I had not,
I had to stay mute

before the possibility of time I was lost

Something in a distance occasional chimes iteratively proposing I could bring a new kind of thing near

an unbearable demand that involved sloughing off

understanding of the words that could form around the impression that I was being
    squeezed to death or alternatively invited to unbind myself

Often it is difficult to remember recursively to address the emotion called anger by others drawn, I am, I mean, drawn dramatically into a course of events

with only the most rudimentary sense of what might be accomplished or known

My father was a student of patriarchy thus wasted some part of considerable genius

Yet he gathered

To raise his girl children as men, an act of love

The residual estrangement and sexual Impossibility he began to understand quite late; already he was dying

when advices or odors of retreat came into his language he was panicking about

the space of isolation he saw forming around me how it was impossible for me to

Understand words outside of fucking

when they were coming to men / how they made no sense

there was no urban gesture of a black man i could fail to understand as i had been taught

We were together in a certain prismatic form of being lettered

Such as the intestinal decay i perceived on him before the diagnosis of pancreatic cancer

See, it is so difficult to stay naming the situation I intend, "anger" laughable in its failure

to reflect being at least among the persons here, among those loved, "anger" springing

up relentlessly to cover over the truth

enumerating the transports of being loved and hated as an obvious and embodied

problem of art, on that, the problem the properties of this music, which has none of the

features ascribed to it because ascription is the problem

The considerable genius of many persons passes over me as I sleep
cancers take me, i lose my crystal vessels, other talismanic objects i keep around to a ne-
glectful curator of African AMerican family history, i am distinctly and rightly paranoid
about oncoming institutions
I have so little time to get my son upright before i am no more
Or extinguished by the humor i find in stuff like downward class mobility

Urgently experiencing negative divisibility, i cannot picture it to you
Composing on Pope.L a little treatise comes into my mind on "nigger-in-the-title"
materiality
Also:
"Washed Up: Future and the problem of diminishing longevity"
All distances in space and time are shrinking—Martin Heidegger
I am not humorless. I am amused by the necessity of reading Heidegger because I can
     read. In the same way I am able to love a man because I can love.
No one says, we can be safe together because we are together. This is where there is next
to go / what I am struggling to get to.
The torment of experiencing the fullness of imagination outside form is this right this
problematic of possible injury the certainty of it unto the end of this order where every
foray into vision is an occasion for attack
there is no philosophical language for the balm of this injury and horror of its recession
the durational poverty of seeing I point to this other place of ongoing work, but they
will just want to watch the thing happen or make me make it happen for them but if you
don't want to get hurt you can't be in it